MARTIN INFANTS' SCHOOL,
HIGH ROAD
EAST FINCHLEY, N.2
01-883-1455

WITHDRAWN

D1792732

Books in the Linkers series

Homes discovered through Art & Technology
Homes discovered through Geography
Homes discovered through History
Homes discovered through Science

Myself discovered through Art & Technology
Myself discovered through Geography
Myself discovered through History
Myself discovered through Science

Toys discovered through Art & Technology
Toys discovered through Geography
Toys discovered through History
Toys discovered through Science

Water discovered through Art & Technology
Water discovered through Geography
Water discovered through History
Water discovered through Science

First paperback edition 1996
First published 1996 in hardback by A&C Black (Publishers) Limited
35 Bedford Row, London WC1R 4JH

ISBN 0-7136-4592-X
A CIP catalogue record for this book is available from the British Library.

Copyright © 1996 BryantMole Books

Commissioned photographs by Zul Mukhida
Design by Jean Wheeler   Picture research by Liz Harman

Acknowledgements

Advertising Archives; 11 (right), 21, Beamish; 3 (right), 6/7, 8, 10, 13 (right), 15 (both), 16, 17 (both), 19 (right), 20 (right), 22 (both), Cephas; 13 (left), Mary Evans Picture Library; 2, Hulton-Deutsch Collection; 3 (left), 5 (both), 11 (left), 12, National Waterways Archives; 13 (right), Robert Opie; 19 (left), 20 (left), Positive Images; 9 (left), Topham; 4 and cover, 9 (right), Tony Stone; John Edwards 23, Zefa; 14.

All rights reserved. No part of this publication may be reproduced in any form or by any means – graphic, electronic or mechanical, including photocopying, recording, taping or information storage and retrieval systems – without the prior permission in writing of the publishers.

Printed and bound in Italy by L.E.G.O.

Water

discovered through
History

Karen Bryant-Mole

Contents

Water 2
Sail power 4
From steam to diesel 6
Crossing the seas 8
The navy 10
Rivers and canals 12
Water power 14
Water in our homes 16
Getting washed 18
Wash day 20
Waste water 22
Glossary 24
Index 24
Timeline 25

A & C Black • London

Water

Water has played an important part in our history.

Explorers
Many years ago, people had little idea of what the world looked like.

Explorers travelled across the seas to discover other lands.

Viking explorers, like those in the drawing below, sailed the seas over a thousand years ago.

History

Water has shaped our history in many ways.
We have used it to power machines.
We have travelled across it and fought battles on it.

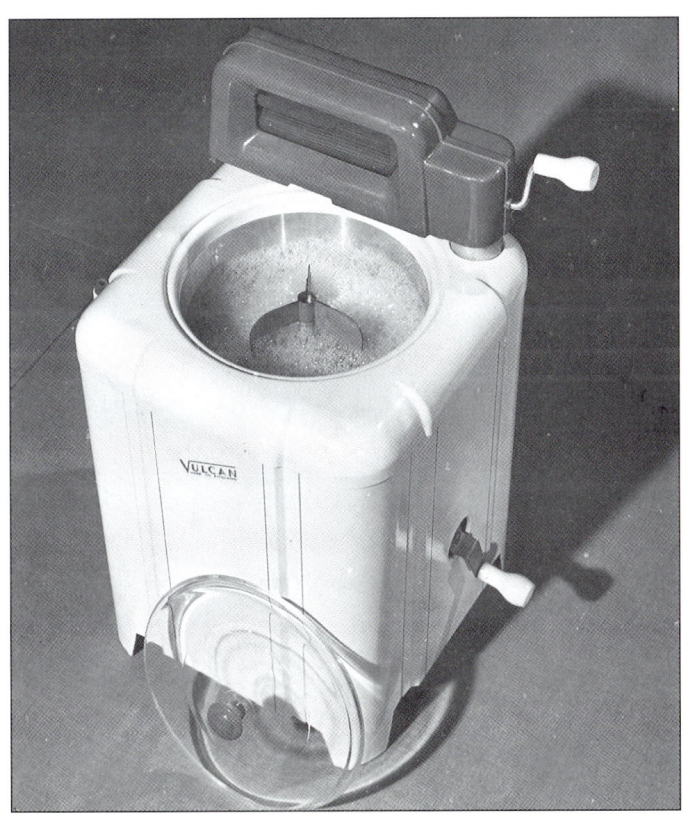

Homes

We have found different ways of using water at home.
We have washed our clothes and bodies with it.
We have found new ways of bringing fresh water into our homes.

This book looks at the history of water during the past one hundred years.

Sail power

Before engines were invented, almost all ships were sailing ships.

Sailing ships
Ships like this one were a common sight one hundred years ago.
Today, there are very few of them left.

Sailing ships were pushed along by the wind.
In strong winds, there was a danger of being blown the wrong way.
In light winds, the ship could not travel very fast.

Yachts

Sail power can be used for fun. Sailors have always enjoyed racing their yachts.
This picture of a yacht race was taken in 1932.

Travel

Some sailors have travelled all the way around the world in a yacht.
In 1977, Dame Naomi James became one of the first women to sail a yacht round the world on her own.

From steam to diesel

The first engines in ships used steam to turn the ship's propeller.
Engines were more reliable than wind power.

Coal
Eighty years ago, many ships were powered by steam.
The steam came from boiling water, which was heated by coal fires.
Ships had to be loaded with coal before each journey.

Diesel
This ship, which was built in 1953, was powered by diesel engines.
Today, almost all ships have diesel engines.

Mauretania
The steam ship in the picture above is the Mauretania. From 1909 to 1929, it held the record for being the fastest ship to cross the Atlantic Ocean, taking just four days, ten hours.

Crossing the seas

The ships that cross the world's seas have carried both people and goods.

Goods
For many hundreds of years, traders have sold goods to other countries.
These goods are often transported by ship.

This picture was taken fifty years ago.
A train is being loaded on to the ship.
Today, a ship might carry computers or cars.

New life

The children in the picture on the right are travelling across the sea with their family, to start a new life in a different country. This is called emigrating.

During the 1940s, 1950s and 1960s, many British families emigrated to countries like America, Canada and Australia.

Holidays

These children are going on holiday by boat. The picture was taken nearly thirty years ago.

Today, journeys across the sea are often made by plane.

The navy

The navy is the name given to a country's fighting ships and the people that work on them.

Warships
Warships have to be able to attack ships, planes and even submarines.

HMS Princess Royal was built in 1910. As well as having guns above water, it could fire torpedoes under the water.

Wars
During wars, battles are often fought at sea as well as on land. This picture shows a British naval ship sinking after it had been bombed during World War II.

Joining up
Navies protect their countries and can be called on to fight.

This 1940s poster is encouraging people to join the American navy. In times of peace, as well as war, many men and women choose to have a job in the navy.

Rivers and canals

Rivers and canals used to play an important part in the transport of goods.

Rivers
A hundred years ago, sailing boats, like this barge, were a common sight on rivers.
They delivered their goods to warehouses on the riverside.

The direction of the wind sometimes meant that sailing boats had to zigzag their way up the river.

Canals

Unlike rivers, canals had to be built. They passed through important towns and connected up with rivers, so that goods could be carried all over the country.
Canal boats were pulled by horses who walked along a path next to the canal.

Today

Today, it is usually quicker to send goods around the country by road or rail. Canals are now popular for holidays. People enjoy travelling slowly through the countryside in barges and other types of boats.

Water power

When water was turned into steam it could be used to power many different machines.

Trains
Steam engines were used to power trains. As the train travelled along, coal was shovelled into a hot fire to heat water and make steam.
Water tanks were built next to the tracks, so that trains always had enough water.

Today, trains like these are often used as tourist attractions.

Vehicles

Steam engines were used to power heavy working vehicles, such as steam rollers and traction engines.

Traction engines were used on farms for jobs such as harvesting.

Today, combine harvesters do this work.

Factories

Steam could also be used to work machines in factories.

Steam was used at this factory to power special machines called lathes.

Water in our homes

Today, most people just turn on the tap when they want water. In the past, getting water was not so easy.

Water carriers
This picture was taken a hundred years ago. The man was a water carrier.
He collected water from a well and travelled around selling it to people.

Pumps

Eighty years ago, many people got their water from a water pump.
A handle at the back had to be pulled up and pushed down.
The water gushed out of the spout.
It then had to be carried home.

Pipes

This picture was taken seventy years ago.
It shows men laying water pipes, which would bring water right into people's homes.

Piped water made a big difference to people's everyday lives.

Getting washed

Getting washed in a bathroom is quite a new idea.

Bowl and jug
A hundred years ago, you might have had a bowl and jug like this in your bedroom.

Hot water was brought up from the kitchen in the jug. It was then tipped into the bowl, ready for someone to have a wash.

Bath

The picture on the right was taken recently, in a museum.
In the past, many people used to wash in a tin bath like this.
It must have been very difficult to get clean if you had a dirty job, such as mining.

Bathrooms

By the 1930s, most new homes were built with bathrooms.
Lots of homes still only had cold water taps.
Special tanks, called geysers, were sometimes used to heat up water for the bath.

Wash day

We use water to clean our clothes.

Wash day
A hundred years ago, most people used a wash tub and washing dolly. In this picture, one woman is using the dolly to swish the clothes around in the soapy water.
The other woman is rinsing the clothes and wringing out the water.

Soap
Clothes were usually washed with a bar of soap.
The same soap could be used to clean floors and wash dishes.
Today, most people use washing powder to wash their clothes.

Washing machines
Washing machines have made washing clothes much quicker and easier.

This machine is about thirty years old.
It is called a twin tub.
The clothes were washed in one side of the machine and spun in the other.

Waste water

Water that has been used in our homes is known as waste water.

Open drains
The picture below was taken in the 1900s.
The boy is tipping waste water into an open drain.
Open drains were often smelly.
Germs from dirty drains could cause diseases.

Sewage
The waste that comes from the toilet is called sewage.
A hundred years ago, most people only had an outside toilet.
The waste usually went into a tank.
This man collected the waste in his cart.

Pipes

Today, the waste water from our homes is taken away, through underground pipes, to a water treatment plant like the one in this picture.

Here, the water is cleaned before being piped back into rivers.

By taking care of water in this way, we are looking after one of the world's most important materials.

Glossary

Atlantic Ocean The ocean between Europe and North America
goods things that are made or grown and then sold
lathes machines that are used to shape wood or metal
materials what things are made from
naval to do with the navy
propeller an object with blades that whirl round
reliable can be depended on
torpedo an object rather like a huge underwater bullet
trader someone who buys or sells goods
warehouses large buildings where goods are stored

Index

bathrooms 18, 19
battles 3, 11
boats 12, 13
canals 13
coal 6, 14
diesel 7
emigrating 9
engines 4, 6–7
explorers 2
factories 15
goods 8
holidays 9, 13
homes 3, 16–17, 18, 19
James, Dame Naomi 5
machines 3
navies 10–11
rivers 12
sailing 4–5
ships 4–5, 6–7, 8–9, 10, 11
soap 20
steam 6, 7, 14–15
toilets 22
trains 14
vehicles 14, 15
Vikings 2
warships 10
washing 3, 18–19, 20–21
washing dollies 20
washing machines 21
waste water 22–23
water carriers 16
water pumps 17

How to use this book

Each book in this series takes a familiar topic or theme and focuses on one area of the curriculum: science, art and technology, geography or history. The books are intended as starting points, illustrating some of the many different angles from which a topic can be studied. They should act as springboards for further investigation, activity or information seeking.

The following list of books may prove useful.

Further books to read

Series	Title	Author	Publisher
Beginner's Knowledge	Ships, Sailors and the Sea	Young & Miles	Usborne
Explainers	Things that Float	A. Thomas	Usborne
	Travel and Transport Long Ago	H. Edom	
History from Objects	Keeping Clean	K. Bryant-Mole	Wayland
History Mysteries	Bathtime	Tanner & Wood	A&C Black
	Washing		
People through History	People at Home	K. Bryant-Mole	Wayland
See Through History	Submarines and Ships	R. Humble	Heinemann
Timelines	Ships	R. Humble	Watts

Timeline

You can use this timeline to work out how long ago the things in this book were made and to compare the ages of different items.

nearly 120 years ago	nearly 110 years ago	nearly 100 years ago	nearly 90 years ago	nearly 80 years ago	nearly 70 years ago	nearly 60 years ago	nearly 50 years ago	nearly 40 years ago	nearly 30 years ago	nearly 20 years ago	nearly 10 years ago
the 1880s	the 1890s	the 1900s	the 1910s	the 1920s	the 1930s	the 1940s	the 1950s	the 1960s	the 1970s	the 1980s	the 1990s
1880	1890	1900	1910	1920	1930	1940	1950	1960	1970	1980	1990